D0467402

LIFE'S LITTLE
TREASURE BOOK

*On
Joy*

H. JACKSON BROWN, JR.

RUTLEDGE HILL PRESS
NASHVILLE, TENNESSEE

Published in Nashville, Tennessee, by
Rutledge Hill Press, Inc., 211 Seventh Avenue
North, Nashville, Tennessee 37219.
Distributed in Canada by H. B. Fenn and
Company Ltd., Mississauga, Ontario.

Typography by D&T/Bailey Typesetting, Inc.,
Nashville, Tennessee
Illustrations by Cristine Mortensen
Book design by Harriette Bateman

ISBN: 1-55853-278-1

Printed in Hong Kong through Palace Press
1 2 3 4 5 6 7 8 9 — 97 96 95 94

INTRODUCTION

One of life's great discoveries is that joy comes from the enjoyment and appreciation of simple things—the sun on your face, the sound of children's laughter, rereading your favorite book. But the true essence of joy is found in giving. We experience the greatest joy when we create it for others.

Casare Pavese reminds us that we do not remember days, we remember moments. And a sure way to create a treasured moment is to bring joy to another heart. A phone call to an old friend, tucking a love note in your child's lunch box, feeding a stranger's expired parking meter are thoughtful and loving actions that create joy for both giver and receiver.

This little book is a collection of joyful ideas that I shared with my son, Adam, in both volumes of *Life's Little Instruction Book*. I hope there are some you might want to try.

And should the entry on page 19 catch your eye, here's a suggestion:

make two pans of brownies and share
one with a neighbor. Eating brownies
makes us happy, sharing brownies
makes us joyful. There is a difference.

Compliment three people
every day.

∾

Always have something
beautiful in sight, even if it's
just a daisy in a jelly glass.

∾

Surprise an old friend with a
phone call.

$\mathcal{D}$on't overlook
life's small joys while
searching for the big ones.

❧

$\mathcal{T}$ake a kid to the zoo.

❧

$\mathcal{E}$njoy tomato soup and
a toasted cheese sandwich.

$\mathcal{M}$ake someone's day
by paying the toll
for the person
in the car behind you.

*T*ravel. See new places, but
remember to take along
an open mind.

❧

*V*olunteer to be a
little league umpire.

❧

*E*njoy real maple syrup.

$\mathcal{W}$hen a waitress or waiter
provides exceptional service,
leave a generous tip,
plus a short note such as,
"Thanks for the wonderful
service. You made our meal a
special experience."

*Great joy, especially
after a sudden change
of circumstances,
is apt to be silent, and
dwells rather in the heart
than on the tongue.*

— Henry Fielding

$\mathcal{S}$treet musicians are
a treasure, stop for a
moment and listen;
then leave a small donation.

❧

$\mathcal{R}$ub a dog's belly.

❧

$\mathcal{H}$ug a cow.

$\mathcal{B}$uy whatever
kids are selling on card tables
in their front yards.

❧

$\mathcal{W}$atch the movie,
Grand Canyon.

$\mathcal{G}$o to a county fair
and check out the
4-H Club exhibits.
It will renew your faith
in the younger generation.

❧

$\mathcal{O}$rder a seed catalog.
Read it on the day of
the first snowfall.

Count

your

blessings.

Slow dance.

❧

Help a child plant a
small garden.

❧

If your town has
a baseball team,
attend the season opener.

*M*ake a pan of brownies.
Lick the spoon.

∽

*R*ead to a child his or her
favorite nursery rhyme.

∽

*W*hen you feel terrific,
notify your face.

$\mathcal{N}$ever be ashamed of
laughter that's too loud or
singing that's too joyful.

❧

$\mathcal{I}$f you make a lot of money,
put it to use helping others
while you are living.
That is wealth's
greatest satisfaction.

Give thanks before every meal.

✺

"*On with the dance!*
let joy be unconfined"
is my motto, whether
there's any dance to dance
or joy to unconfine.

— Mark Twain

*L*ife is short.
Eat more pancakes
and fewer
rice cakes.

$\mathcal{L}$earn to make
great spaghetti sauce.
Your mother's recipe is
the best.

∾

$\mathcal{G}$et a car with a sun roof.

∾

$\mathcal{H}$ave a dog.

When renting a car for a couple of days, splurge and get the big Lincoln.

❧

One can endure sorrow alone, but it takes two to be glad.

— Elbert Hubbard

$\mathcal{G}$ive someone a backrub.

$\mathcal{H}$ave someone give
you a backrub.

*L*earn to show cheerfulness,
even when you don't
feel like it.

∾

*L*earn to show enthusiasm,
even when you don't
feel like it.

Skip one meal a week
and give what you
would have spent to
a street person.

❧

Take a kid roller skating.

❧

Sing in the shower.

Attend class reunions.

∾

Drink champagne for
no reason at all.

∾

Every so often,
go where you can hear a
wooden screen door slam shut.

*L*eave everything
a little better
than you
found it.

Get two goldfish.

✌

Send an anonymous gift
of money to your
favorite charity.

✌

Buy great books even if you
never read them.

*T*our the main branch of
the public library on
Fifth Avenue the next time
you are in New York City.
Unforgettable.

∾

*R*ake a big pile of leaves
every fall and jump in it with
someone you love.

If you would be happy
for a week, take a wife;
if you would be happy
for a month, kill a pig;
but if you would be happy
all your life,
plant a garden.

— Chinese proverb

$\mathcal{L}$earn to identify local
wildflowers, birds, and trees.

∾

$\mathcal{M}$ake yourself some
cinnamon toast.

∾

$\mathcal{R}$ead a book
about beekeeping.

$\mathcal{R}$efrain from envy. It's the source of much unhappiness.

❧

$\mathcal{B}$orrow a box of puppies
for an afternoon and
take them to visit the
residents of a retirement home.
Stand back and
watch the smiles.

$\mathcal{L}$et people
pull in front of you when
you're stopped in traffic.

$\mathcal{P}$ut a love note
in your child's
lunch box.

At the movies,
buy Junior Mints and sprinkle
them on your popcorn.

∾

Whistle.

∾

Wave at children
on school buses.

Write your pastor a note
and tell him how much
he means to you.

∾

Own a cowboy hat.

∾

Own a comfortable chair
for reading.

$\mathcal{T}$ake a kid to visit the local
fire station.

∾

$\mathcal{G}$o to a garage sale.
Buy three things that cost
less than a dollar each.

∾

$\mathcal{P}$ray for an enemy.

When traveling
the back roads,
stop whenever you
see a sign
that reads
"Honey for Sale."

*L*earn to identify the music
of Chopin, Mozart,
and Beethoven.

❧

*T*each some kind of class.

❧

*B*e a student in
some kind of class.

$\mathcal{P}$lant flowers every spring.

∾

$\mathcal{F}$orget the Joneses.

∾

$\mathcal{D}$on't waste time trying to
appreciate music you dislike.
Spend the time with music
you love.

$\mathcal{N}$ever miss an opportunity
to ride a roller coaster.

∾

$\mathcal{R}$ead the Sunday paper in a
hammock. Then take a nap.

∾

$\mathcal{M}$ake new friends
but cherish the old ones.

$\mathcal{T}$est drive a fast,
red sports car.

∾

$\mathcal{W}$rite a note of appreciation
to one of your favorite
teachers from long ago and
tell him or her the difference
he or she made
in your life.

*E*very once in
a while,
take the
scenic route.

$\mathcal{G}$o to Home Depot and just look around.

❧

$\mathcal{L}$earn to play a musical instrument.

❧

$\mathcal{T}$ake a nap on Sunday afternoons.

Live your life as
an exclamation,
not an explanation.

∽

A merry heart
does good,
like medicine.

— Proverbs 17:22

Own a great stereo system.

❧

Watch the movie
It's A Wonderful Life
every Christmas.

❧

What you must do,
do cheerfully.

*W*ear audacious underwear under the most solemn business attire.

∾

*G*et your car washed.

∾

*G*et your spouse's car washed.

$\mathcal{P}$repare one of your
grandmother's best recipes;
call her and thank her.

∾

$\mathcal{P}$urchase one piece of
original art each year,
even if it's just a small painting
by a high school student.

Comb your child's hair.

❧

Get your photograph taken
with a friend in one of those
photo booths.

Leave a small gift or
bouquet of flowers on
someone's desk at work.

∾

Oh, how good it feels!
The hand of an old friend.

— Henry Wadsworth Longfellow

When visiting a small town
at lunch time,
choose the café
on the square.

Go to rodeos.

Work in a garden.

*L*earn to make
something beautiful
with your hands.

$\mathcal{L}$ife will sometimes
hand you a magical moment.
Savor it.

∾

$\mathcal{B}$uy raffle tickets, candy bars,
and baked goods from
students who are
raising money for
school projects.

Read more books.

❧

Watch less TV.

❧

Happiness is an
inside job.

— Horace Brown

Once every couple of months
enjoy a four-course meal —
only eat each course at a
different restaurant.

∾

Every so often,
invite the person
in line behind you
to go ahead of you.

*A*ttend a high school
football game.
Sit near the band.

∾

*S*pread crunchy
peanut butter on
Pepperidge Farm Gingerman
cookies for the perfect
late-night snack.

Smile a lot.
It costs nothing and
is beyond price.

*W*ave to crosswalk
patrol mothers.

❧

*N*ever laugh at
anyone's dreams.

❧

*G*o to a greeting card display
and read the humorous cards.

$\mathcal{V}$isit your old high school
and introduce yourself to
the principal.
Ask if you can sit in on a
couple of classes.

$\mathcal{W}$rite your favorite author
a note of appreciation.

Learn to make great chili.

❧

Tape record your
parents' laughter.

*To be without
some of the things you
want is an indispensable
part of happiness.*

— Bertrand Russell

$\mathcal{S}$end someone you love a
copy of Under My Elm
by David Grayson
(Renaissance House, 1986).

❧

$\mathcal{C}$all home.

❧

$\mathcal{T}$reat yourself to
an extravagant dessert.

*O*nce in your life
own a convertible.

❧

*Happiness?
That's nothing more
than good health and
a poor memory.*

— Albert Schweitzer

*O*vertip

breakfast

waitresses.

$\mathcal{G}$o home for the holidays.

⌒

$\mathcal{P}$ay for a needy child to
go to summer camp.

⌒

$\mathcal{P}$ut a lot of little
marshmallows in your
hot chocolate.

$\mathcal{B}$uy three best-selling
children's books.
Read them and then
give them to a youngster.

∾

$\mathcal{T}$ake an overnight
train trip and
sleep in a Pullman.

*T*ake your
best friend to lunch.

∽

*P*atronize drug stores
with soda fountains.

∽

*S*end all of your cousins
a greeting card.

*J*ust for fun,
attend a small-town
Fourth of July celebration.

∾

*G*o through all
your old photographs.
Select ten and tape them
to your kitchen cabinets.
Change them every
thirty days.

Occasionally in life there are those moments of unutterable fulfillment which cannot be completely explained by those symbols called words. Their meanings can only be articulated by the inaudible language of the heart.

— Martin Luther King, Jr.

$\mathcal{G}$o to chili cook-offs.

❧

$\mathcal{J}$oin a slow-pitch
softball league.

❧

$\mathcal{L}$earn to play
"Amazing Grace"
on the piano.

$\mathcal{L}$augh a lot.
A good sense of humor cures
almost all of life's ills.

❧

$\mathcal{S}$eek out the
good in people.

❧

$\mathcal{T}$ake time to smell the roses.

$\mathcal{I}$'ve never seen
a smiling face
that wasn't
beautiful.

— Unknown

$\mathcal{W}$atch a sunrise
at least once a year.

∾

$\mathcal{E}$very so often let your spirit
of adventure triumph over
your good sense.

∾

$\mathcal{L}$earn to bake bread.

$\mathscr{M}$ake it a habit to
do nice things for
people who will
never find out.

∾

$\mathscr{W}$hen boarding a bus,
say "hello" to the driver.
Say "thank you" when
you get off.

$\mathcal{L}$ie on your back and
look at the stars.

∾

$\mathcal{H}$e is happiest,
be he king or peasant,
who finds peace
in his home.

— Goethe

$\mathcal{B}$egin each day with
your favorite music.

∾

$\mathcal{D}$on't let your possessions
possess you.

∾

$\mathcal{L}$ove someone who
doesn't deserve it.

$\mathcal{R}$ead a chapter or two from
Chicken Soup for the Soul
by Jack Canfield and
Mark Victor Hansen
(Health Communications,
1993).

❧

$\mathcal{T}$ell your boss you
appreciate the opportunity
he or she has given you.

Drop off a pizza at the
local police station.

❧

Take a bubble bath with
soft candlelight and
your favorite music.

❧

Be the first to say "Hello."

*R*emember that
what you give
will afford you
more pleasure than
what you get.

*O*nce a year, go someplace
you've never been before.

❧

*M*emorize your favorite
love poem.

❧

*G*ive a pint of blood.

$\mathcal{L}$earn three knock-knock
jokes so you will
always be ready to
entertain children.

∞

$\mathcal{B}$uy a small,
inexpensive camera.
Take it with you
everywhere.

*B*uy a bird feeder and
hang it so that you can
see it from your
kitchen window.

∾

*L*ie on the floor with
a new set of 64 crayons and a
coloring book.
Color your troubles away.

$\mathcal{L}$earn to juggle.

❧

$\mathcal{T}$ake a brisk
thirty-minute walk
every day.

❧

$\mathcal{U}$se a favorite picture of a
loved one as a bookmark.

*A*ttach a small
Christmas wreath to
your car's grill
on the
first day of December.

∾

*R*emember that
half the joy of achievement
is in the anticipation.

$\mathcal{P}$lant a tree

on your

birthday.

*C*hoose a church that
sings joyful music.

∾

*T*reat yourself to a massage
on your birthday.

Never acquire
just one kitten.
Two are a lot more fun and
no more trouble.

∾

When you see
visitors taking pictures
of each other,
offer to take a picture of
their group together.

$\mathcal{L}$eave a quarter where a
child can find it.

❧

$\mathcal{L}$earn three clean jokes.

❧

$\mathcal{W}$atch reruns of
"The Andy Griffith Show."

*T*ake lots of snapshots.

❧

*W*rite your child's teacher
a note of appreciation.

❧

*F*eed a stranger's
expired parking meter.

$\mathcal{S}$ing in a choir.

❧

$\mathcal{F}$ly Old Glory
on the
Fourth of July.

❧

$\mathcal{T}$reat everyone you meet
like you want to be treated.

*U*nderstand that
happiness is not based on
possessions, power,
or prestige,
but on relationships with
people you
love and respect.

∾

*D*on't postpone joy.